P9-BYJ-897

For those who like the record set straight —T. L. S.

Henry Holt and Company, *Publishers since 1866*
Henry Holt® is a registered trademark of Macmillan Publishing Group, LLC
120 Broadway, New York, NY 10271 • mackids.com

Library of Congress Cataloging-in-Publication Data
Names: Stone, Tanya Lee, author. | Salerno, Steven, illustrator.
Title: Pass go and collect $200 : the real story of how Monopoly was invented /
Tanya Lee Stone ; illustrations by Steven Salerno.
Description: First edition. | New York : Henry Holt and Company, 2018 |
"Christy Ottaviano Books." | Includes bibliographical references. |
Audience: Age 5–9. | Audience: K to Grade 3.
Identifiers: LCCN 2017042615 | ISBN 9781627791687 (hardcover)
Subjects: LCSH: Monopoly (Game)—History—Juvenile literature.
Classification: LCC GV1469.M65 S76 2018 | DDC 794—dc23
LC record available at https://lccn.loc.gov/2017042615

Our books may be purchased in bulk for promotional, educational, or business use.
Please contact your local bookseller or the Macmillan Corporate and Premium Sales Department at
(800) 221-7945 ext. 5442 or by e-mail at MacmillanSpecialMarkets@macmillan.com.

First edition, 2018 / Designed by Patrick Collins
The artist created the original illustrations for this book with crayon, ink, gouache, and pastel on paper. After scanning the drawings, he layered and arranged them into the final compositions using Adobe Photoshop, with additional coloring applied.
Printed in China by RR Donnelley Asia Printing Solutions Ltd., Dongguan City, Guangdong Province

5 7 9 10 8 6

PASS GO

AND COLLECT $200

THE REAL STORY OF HOW MONOPOLY WAS INVENTED

Tanya Lee Stone

illustrated by Steven Salerno

Christy Ottaviano Books

HENRY HOLT AND COMPANY ✦ NEW YORK

SHORT LINE R.R
Chest
DVANCE TO GO
(COLLECT $200)
Chance
PAY
POOR TAX
OF $15
ELECTRIC COMPANY
$75.

What kind of Monopoly player are YOU? Do you save your money until you land on Park Place or Boardwalk? Do you buy up all the properties you can? Do you always want to be the banker? Do you and your friends like to make the game last for days—or find ways to play a shorter game?

Monopoly is one of the most famous games in the world. More than one billion people have played it in 111 countries. One BILLION!

Monopoly is really about making and losing money. The person with the most money and property at the end of the game wins. Have you ever wondered who invented Monopoly? Or how rich and famous that person became? Was the inventor of Monopoly the ultimate winner? We need to look back more than a hundred years to find out.

Lizzie Magie
(1866–1948)

Elizabeth Magie—or Lizzie, as she was called—was a woman of many talents. She was smart, made people laugh easily, wrote poetry and short stories, and enjoyed acting. Sometimes Lizzie would dress in a costume, knock on her own door, and trick her husband into thinking she was someone else! She wasn't afraid to speak her mind publicly, either, which was brave behavior for a woman at the time. Perhaps the most important thing about Lizzie Magie, though, was that she took issues of fairness quite seriously.

In the late 1800s, millions of Americans left small towns and farming areas to move to cities, where workers were needed more than ever before. Of course, they had to have places to live. A small number of wealthy people began to buy as much land as they could and build houses and apartment buildings. They charged people fees, or rent, to live there. The more land the owners controlled, the higher the rent increased. This created a situation in which the landlords could become wealthier while renters, or tenants, stayed poor.

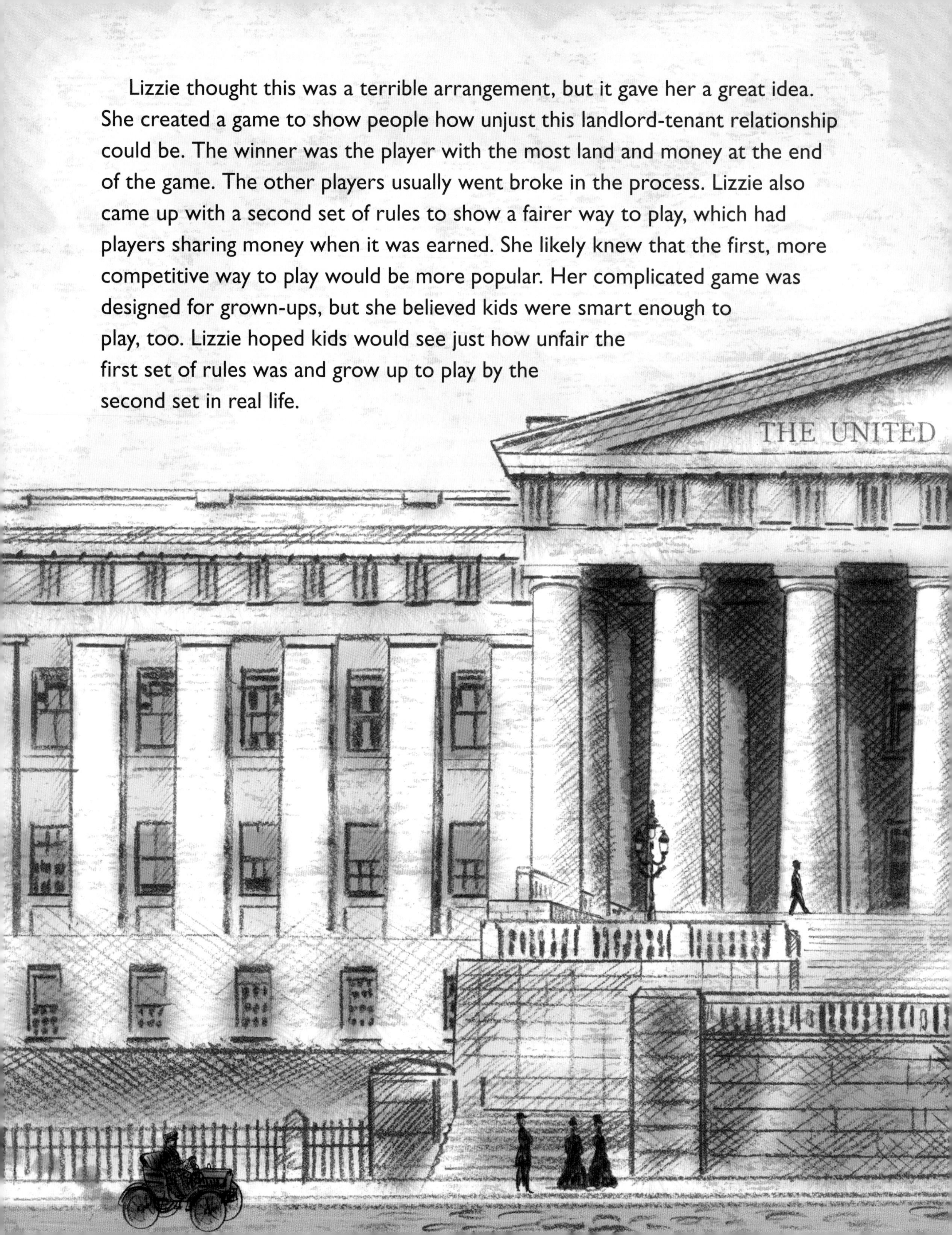

Lizzie thought this was a terrible arrangement, but it gave her a great idea. She created a game to show people how unjust this landlord-tenant relationship could be. The winner was the player with the most land and money at the end of the game. The other players usually went broke in the process. Lizzie also came up with a second set of rules to show a fairer way to play, which had players sharing money when it was earned. She likely knew that the first, more competitive way to play would be more popular. Her complicated game was designed for grown-ups, but she believed kids were smart enough to play, too. Lizzie hoped kids would see just how unfair the first set of rules was and grow up to play by the second set in real life.

Lizzie Magie called it the Landlord's Game, and in 1903, she filed a patent to claim credit for her invention. Lizzie's patent detailed her game rules and included a drawing of the board and its pieces. It was the first time anyone had ever filed a patent for a board game. The patent was granted in January 1904, at a time when women received fewer than one percent of all US patents.

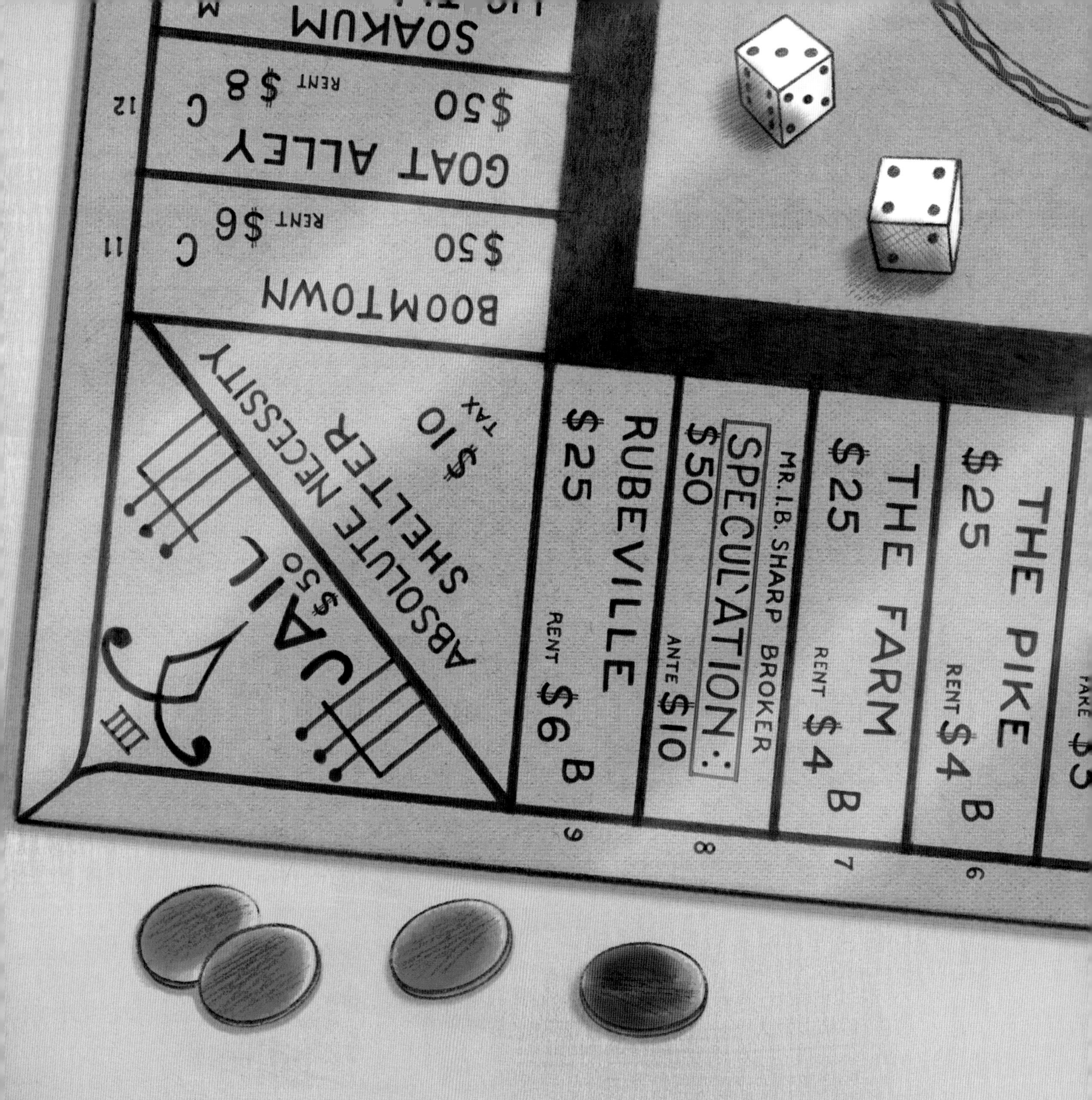

To play her game, Lizzie used dice, a bank with play money, and two kinds of cards—Luxury and Legacy—that a player might draw during a turn. She had four railroads, each one placed in the middle of each side of the board. There were twenty-two properties, or lots, each with a purchase price and a rent value. Any player landing on a lot owned by another player had to pay rent.

Three of the corners on Lizzie's board were labeled Public Park, Go to Jail, and Jail. Players who went to jail had to pay a fine or stay there until they rolled doubles. The fourth corner of Lizzie's board was called Mother Earth. Each time players passed Mother Earth, completing one turn around the board, they collected $100.

Does any of this sound familiar?

Lizzie Magie kept improving her game, designing a new board in 1906. She and two friends manufactured a small number of them. Lizzie added some new rules, including charging more rent for owning multiple railroads. Fans of the game also started using handmade boards. Pretty soon, lots of people were playing her game.

One of them was a man named Scott Nearing. He taught business at the University of Pennsylvania and took Lizzie's game to class to teach his students about landlords and rent. He and his students loved the game. They started calling it Monopoly because that's the term used when an owner gains sole control over a group of properties.

The students made replicas of the game. They shared them with other students at other colleges. The Landlord's Game was probably the most complex game of its time, but people enjoyed its many ideas and rules. Word spread, and soon more and more people were playing Lizzie Magie's game—although most didn't know it was her idea.

Do you ever change the rules when you play Monopoly with your friends? Well, that's what was happening with Lizzie's game. It became common for people to make their own boards—often adding local street names—and tweak the rules to their liking.

Scott Nearing
(1883–1983)

The Parker Brothers Game Company
Charles H. Parker
(1860–1936)
George S. Parker
(1866–1952)
Edward H. Parker
(1855–1915)

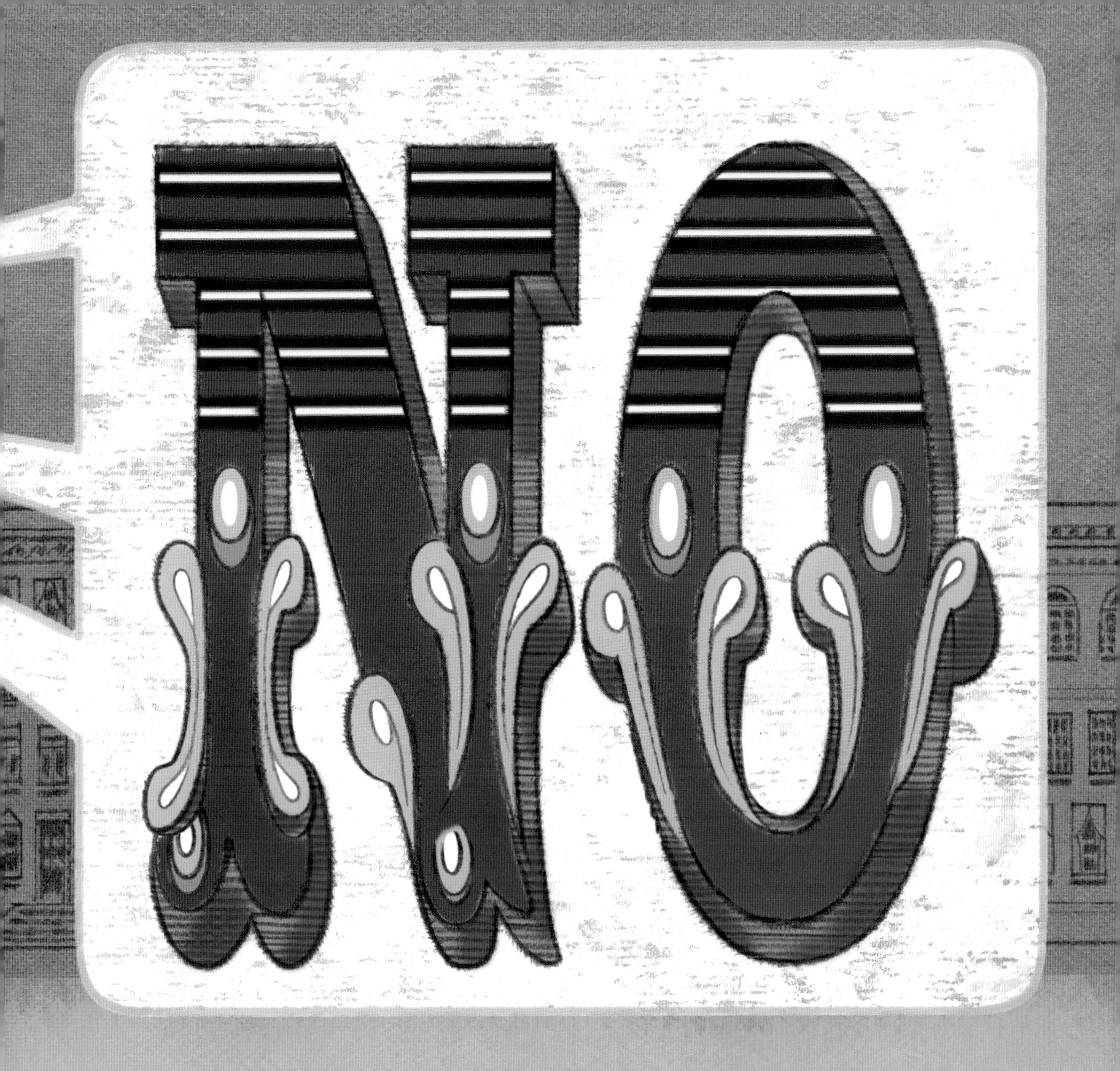

In 1909, Lizzie Magie showed her game board to George Parker. George and his two brothers owned the Parker Brothers game company. They admired her game, but they thought it was too challenging and educational. They turned her down. She made more changes and tried to sell her game to Parker Brothers again, but they still weren't interested. In 1924, Lizzie renewed her patent. This time, she added a rule that allowed a player who owned all railroads or utilities to double the rent. And her "Improvements" rule allowed players to add houses to their property, increasing the rent.

None of this stopped Lizzie's game from continuing to attract new players. Devoted fans kept making their own changes. The most lasting changes happened in Atlantic City, New Jersey, in 1930. Ruth Hoskins, a young Quaker teacher, and her friends renamed most of the properties after Atlantic City streets and neighborhoods. They were inspired by locations such as St. Charles Place, Ventnor Avenue, and Boardwalk. Someone else came up with color sequences and dividing the properties into groups of three. Atlantic City players added hotels to the game as well.

Around this time, a huge financial crisis called the Great Depression struck. All across the country, companies and farms went out of business; people had trouble paying for everything from food to rent. By 1932, one in four Americans had lost their jobs. One of them was a man named Charles Darrow.

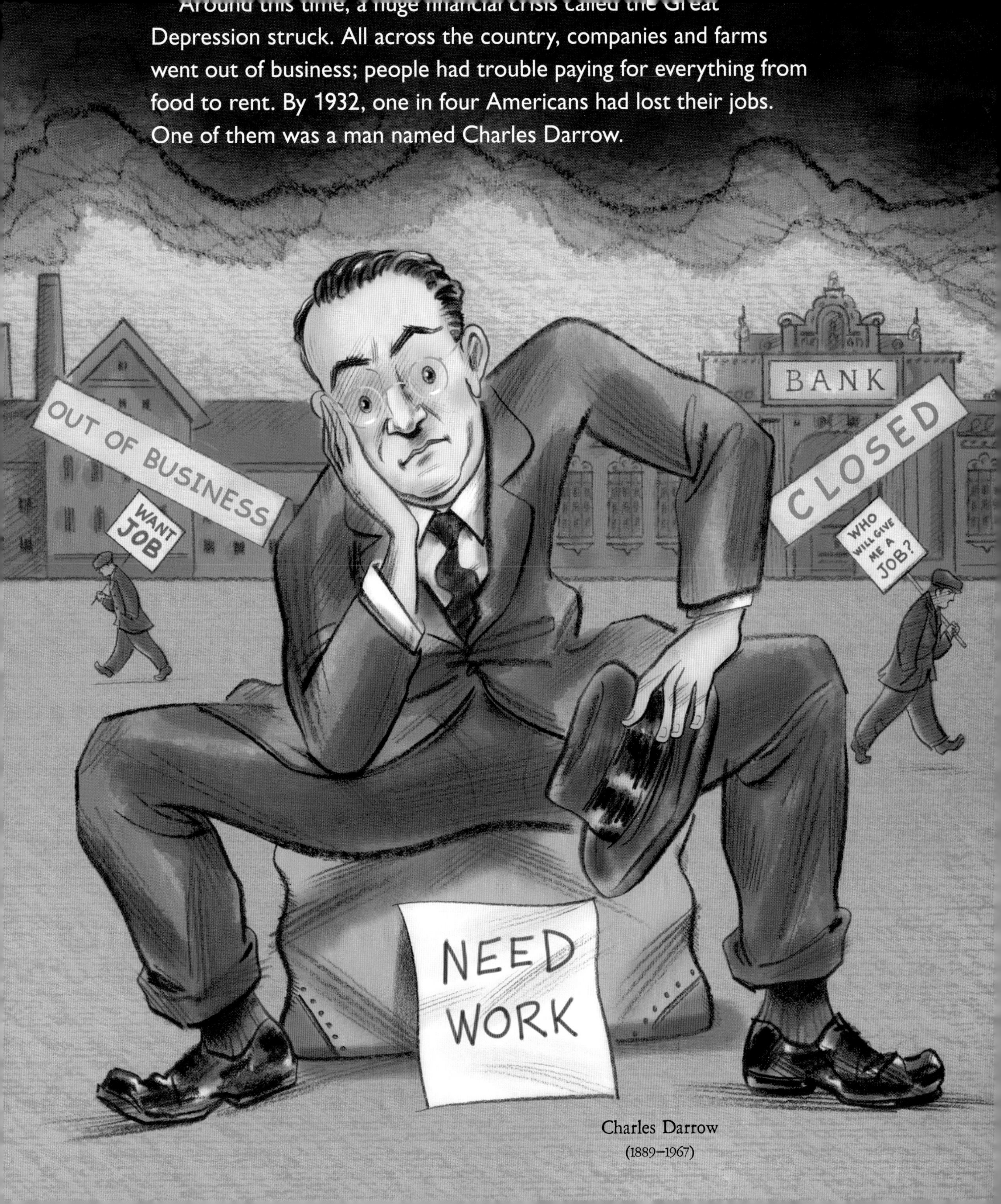

Charles Darrow
(1889–1967)

He and his wife had dinner with friends who happened to have an Atlantic City game board. They taught the Darrows how to play. Charles loved the game and decided to make his own board. He asked his friends for copies of their rules.

You know how some people have a knack for taking something great and making it even better? Well, that's what Charles Darrow did.

The first board he made was round. Although he quickly went back to the idea of a square board, the round one had inspired Charles to draw larger rectangles with bars of color on the top—one for each group of properties. He also created new designs, with the help of stencils, for the Chance question marks, the Water Works faucet, the Electric Company light bulb, and the railroad trains.

Community Chest
Ave.
ELECTRIC COMPANY
CHANCE
RAILROADS
WATER WORKS
CD

Here was another big change—instead of sharing the game freely like most others had done, Charles started selling sets to friends. Nearly broke, he thought it might be a good way to earn money for his family.

He made each one by hand, drawing the game board on a large piece of oilcloth with pen and ink and using oil paint for the colored bands. He cut scraps of wood into houses and hotels and painted those, too. He also typed up the rules. Each game took about eight hours to make. Soon, Charles Darrow advertised his version, claiming credit as its inventor.

MONOPOLY
$2.00
NNECTICUT
AVENUE
Rent
With 1 House
With 2 Houses
With 3 Houses
With 4 Houses
With Hotel
Mortgage Value
The cost of building a house
or hotel is
$50.00
•If all properties of one color
re owned, rent is doubled (on
mproved property only.)
EADING
AIL ROAD
100
50

With some of the profits he earned from selling his sets, Charles paid to have five hundred game boards made by a small local printing firm. He asked a cartoonist friend, Franklin Alexander, to help him improve the look of the game. Franklin added illustrations, such as the Go to Jail police officer and Jake the Jailbird (the man behind the bars). Charles Darrow's colorful board made Monopoly look more dynamic than ever. The 1934 board looks much like the one we know today. On the box, it said simply: MONOPOLY.

Charles tried to sell the game to two companies, one of which was Parker Brothers. He was turned down, just like Lizzie.

But Charles did not give up. He persuaded a big department store and a famous toy store to stock his Monopoly sets for Christmas. Pretty soon, other stores signed on.

TAXI
TAXI

Parker Brothers heard that Charles Darrow's Monopoly game was quickly becoming a big hit. It was selling so well that the "no" Parker Brothers had given him before was about to turn into a "yes." Charles signed a contract with Parker Brothers that included naming him as the game's inventor.

Uh-oh . . . trouble? *You* know that Charles didn't invent Monopoly. Lizzie Magie did! You also know that others made changes to her game as it was passed from community to community across the country. But Charles Darrow's round of changes, his success in selling it, and a new attitude at Parker Brothers finally made the company give Monopoly a chance.

To protect anyone from copying it, Parker Brothers needed a patent. Can you guess what happened next? Parker Brothers discovered Lizzie Magie's patent. George Parker then remembered Lizzie trying to sell him her game years before. After having made an earlier claim that Monopoly was his brainchild, Charles Darrow admitted he had worked from an existing game, but he didn't know who created it.

I'm the inventor!
I'm the inventor!
Chance
INVENT POPULAR GAME,
BECOME MILLIONAIRE

Parker Brothers had a big problem. The company needed to own Lizzie's patent to be able to sell Monopoly. In November 1935, George Parker traveled by train to Lizzie's home to talk with her. He offered her $500 (the equivalent of almost $9,000 today) and promised to publish her original Landlord's Game, as well as two other games she had also invented.

Lizzie Magie agreed, and on the last day of December—more than thirty years after she first invented her board game—Parker Brothers owned all the rights to Monopoly. Charles Darrow was about to become a millionaire.

Wait—what about Lizzie? Charles was going to make millions, and she was getting only $500? The whole reason she invented the Landlord's Game was to show how unfair money issues can become when someone takes sole control over a property.

At first, Lizzie Magie was content with the deal she struck because her ideas would finally reach a mass audience. But she didn't stay content. When Lizzie saw Monopoly for sale in 1936—with Charles Darrow named as its inventor—she was shocked and furious. And she wasn't the only one. Many of the players who added to the game before Charles came along were also upset. Lizzie Magie didn't hesitate to talk to reporters at *The Washington Post.* Although the paper ran a story about Lizzie being the original inventor, the news of her claim eventually faded.

Today, we know that without Lizzie Magie, there likely never would have been a game called Monopoly for us to play and love. Her initial idea is the heart of the game. And without Charles Darrow, Monopoly might not have become America's favorite board game. All the other folks who added their ideas along the way helped make it great, too.

So who wins in this story? What do you think? Did Lizzie Magie make a wrong move? Did Charles Darrow? How would *you* have played it? In any case, there is no doubt that millions of people all over the world adore Monopoly.

SHORT LINE
PLACE
PAY $75.00
PRICE $400
AS YOU PASS
GO
TITLE DEED
MARVIN GARDENS
RENT $24.
With 1 House $ 120.
With 2 Houses 360.
With 3 Houses 850.
With 4 Houses 1025.
With HOTEL $1200.
Mortgage Value $140.
Houses cost $150. each
TITLE DEED
VERMONT

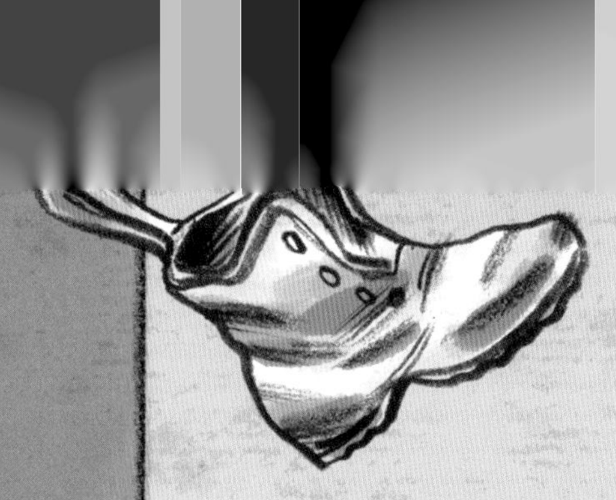
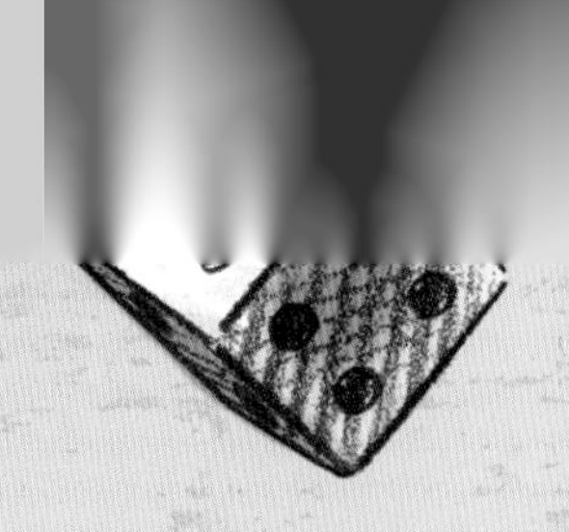

Tremendous Trivia!

- Lizzie Magie also invented a device that helped paper move more easily through typewriter rollers in 1893. That's when she learned how to file a patent.
- During World War II, tokens were made of wood because metal was needed for the war effort.
- In the 1970s, a Braille version of Monopoly was made for the visually impaired.
- People of all ages love Monopoly. A younger version, Monopoly Junior, was introduced in 1990.
- Charles and Olive Todd were the friends who taught Charles Darrow how to play Lizzie's game. The Todds misspelled Atlantic City's real-life suburb Marven Gardens on the board they made, spelling it Marvin Gardens. Darrow copied that misspelling, and it has never been corrected. In 1995, Hasbro (the company that bought Parker Brothers in 1991) apologized to the residents of Marven Gardens.
- Darrow had players use their own tokens, such as charms from girls' bracelets or Cracker Jack boxes. Parker Brothers introduced the metal tokens with their game.
- The longest Monopoly game ever played lasted for 1,680 hours. That's seventy days!
- The character we now call Mr. Monopoly had the name Rich Uncle Pennybags until 1999, and was modeled after famous financier J. P. Morgan.
- Parker Brothers made Darrow the offer to buy Monopoly in the historic Flatiron Building in New York City. Coincidentally, the Flatiron is also where this book was edited and published!
- A worldwide "Save Your Token" campaign on Facebook in 2013 resulted in the iron being retired and a new cat token introduced to the game. In 2017, Hasbro held an online vote to determine the future of some tokens. More than four million people voted. The results retired the boot, thimble, and wheelbarrow and added a penguin, rubber ducky, and T. rex.

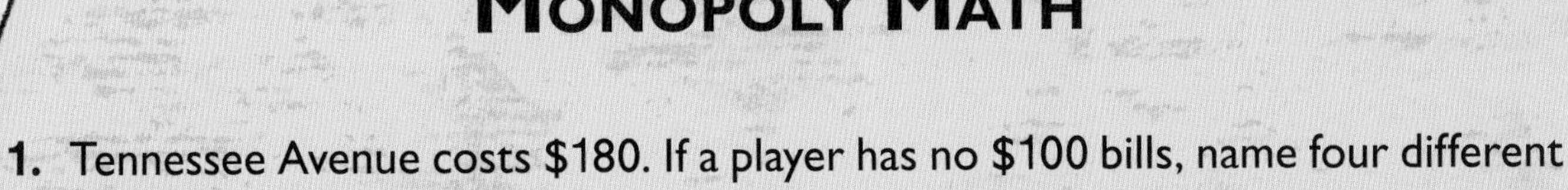

MONOPOLY MATH

1. Tennessee Avenue costs $180. If a player has no $100 bills, name four different ways he or she can pay the banker for this property.

2. If you own 1 utility and someone lands on it, the rent is 4 times what the dice show. If you own both, the rent is 10 times! How much rent do you collect if you only own Water Works and someone lands on it with a roll of double 6s? How much if you own Water Works and Electric Company and a player lands on one with a roll of a 5 and a 3?

3. When you buy all properties in a color set, you have a monopoly. Then you can place houses on them and charge more rent. If three properties cost a total of $320 and houses cost $50 each, and you put 1 house on each property, how much money would you spend? What if you put 3 houses on each property?

4. If someone gives you a $20 bill to pay $8 rent, how many different ways could you make change?

5. For every railroad you own, the rent you charge doubles, starting at $25. If you own 2 railroads, how much rent would you collect? What if you owned all 4?

6. You want to buy Virginia Avenue, which costs $160, but you only have $35. How much more do you need to buy it? Will you be able to buy it the next time you pass Go? Will you have money left over? If so, how much?

MONOPOLY MATH ANSWER KEY

1. Some ways are:
   Three $50s + one $20 + one $10
   Nine $20s
   Eighteen $10s
   Two $50s + four $20s
2. $48, $80
3. $470, $770
4. Twelve $1s
   Two $5s + two $1s
   One $10 + two $1s
   One $5 + seven $1s
5. $50, $200
6. $125. Yes, you will have $75 left over.

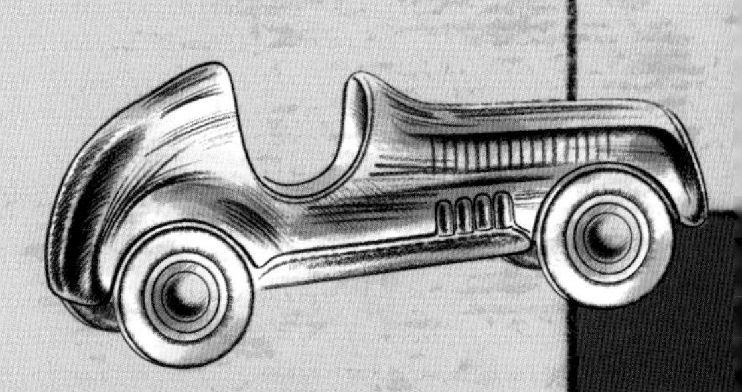

A Note from the Author

One day, my editor Christy Ottaviano asked me if I might be interested in telling the story of how Charles Darrow, an unemployed salesman during the Great Depression, became a millionaire by inventing Monopoly. As she knows I love to discover women's history stories, she simultaneously offered her apologies that this wasn't one, but she thought I would find it intriguing nonetheless. Imagine my surprise, as I researched the game, to find out that it WAS a women's history story. As it turns out, the rags-to-riches tale about Charles Darrow was not quite as it seemed. The man long celebrated as the game's inventor had an important predecessor in Elizabeth "Lizzie" Magie.

It has been a running joke in my family that I seem to keep writing about Elizabeths. (I have written picture books about Elizabeth Cady Stanton and Elizabeth Blackwell.) Once again I was off on another "Elizabeth adventure." It was Lizzie Magie, in fact, who truly invented Monopoly. There's only one kind of story I like as much as a women's history story, and that's a little-known, unsung hero(ine) story—this was both!

As this book goes to press, there is no information about Lizzie Magie on the Hasbro site, although there have been times when Magie's contributions to the game's history were officially noted. Part of the reason the whole complicated history of the game's invention was unearthed and made public was because of a man named Ralph Anspach. He tried to sell a game called Anti-Monopoly in 1974, and Parker Brothers sued him. In preparing his defense, Anspach researched the game's history and studied Lizzie Magie's role in it.

Just as Darrow and others who modified Lizzie's game were inspired by her original idea, it was a writer named Henry George who inspired Lizzie. George's ideas about wealth and poverty caught Lizzie's attention. George believed that everything found in nature—such as land—belonged to everyone and should not be taxed, that the value of land should not rise, and that only what people did to improve the land (such as build on it) should be taxed. Therefore, he reasoned, landowners had no right to continually increase rents simply because they owned the land upon which a building sat. This was the basis of Henry George's single tax theory, and it was this theory that sparked Lizzie Magie to create the Landlord's Game, a game that began the worldwide craze of Monopoly.

Sources

Adams, Cecil. "Monopoly's Anti-Capitalist Origins." *Washington City Paper*, March 18, 2011.

Adams, Charles J., III. "Monopoly: From Berks to Boardwalk." *Historical Review of Berks County*, Winter 1978.

Collins, Doug. "Go to Court, Go Directly to Court." *Washington Free Press*, Nov.–Dec. 1998.

Darrow, C. B. Board game apparatus. U.S. Patent 2,026,082, filed August 31, 1935, and issued December 31, 1935.

Ketcham, Christopher. "Monopoly Is Theft." *Harper's Magazine*, October 19, 2012.

Magie, L. J. Game board. U.S. Patent 748,626, filed March 23, 1903, and issued January 5, 1904.

Orbanes, Philip E. *Monopoly: The World's Most Famous Game & How It Got That Way.* Philadelphia: Da Capo Press, 2006.

———. *The Game Makers: The Story of Parker Brothers from Tiddledy Winks to Trivial Pursuit.* Boston: Harvard Business School Press, 2004.

Pilon, Mary. *The Monopolists: Obsession, Fury, and the Scandal Behind the World's Favorite Board Game.* New York: Bloomsbury, 2015.

———. "Can't Play by the Rules? It's Fine by Mr. Monopoly." *New York Times*, March 25, 2014.

———. "How a Fight Over a Board Game Monopolized an Economist's Life." *The Wall Street Journal*, October 20, 2009.

———. "Monopoly Goes Corporate." *New York Times*, August 24, 2013.

Wolfe, Burton H. "The Monopolization of Monopoly: The $500 Buyout." *The San Francisco Bay Guardian*, 1976.